The Little Book
of Knots and
Splices

The Little Book of Knots and Splices

WAVERLEY BOOKS

First published in this edition 2019,
reprinted 2021 by Waverley Books,
an imprint of The Gresham Publishing Company Ltd,
31, Six Harmony Row,
Glasgow, G51 3BA, Scotland

www.waverley-books.co.uk
info@waverley-books.co.uk
facebook/pages/waverleybooks

ISBN 978-1-84934-505-7

Printed and bound in the EU

Contents

Ropes and Cordage

Until quite recently, rope was made from natural vegetable fibres, most commonly hemp. Currently though, synthetic fibres are generally used for the composition of ropes and cords.

Ropes made from polypropylene fibres are relatively low in cost and are, therefore, commonly used in sailing, other than competitive sailing. Importantly, polypropylene floats well and so is appropriate for use in a wide variety of water-borne activities. Polypropylene is also resistant to abrasion and many of the atmospheric and climatic conditions that can affect the wear of the rope.

Polyamide fibres are favoured for ropes used by climbers because they are strong and elastic. Unlike polypropylene, polyamide does not float but it is used for the fine lines used by fishermen as it lends itself well to holding knots.

Polyester fibres are also used in sailing, although they do not float. This type of rope is highly wear-resistant and has a low-elasticity that can be enhanced in the preparation process to ensure that the rope is not affected by sustained strain.

The most recent development in this area has

been with rope made from aramid fibres, which is extremely strong (its breaking strain is equal to that of steel and almost three times that of vegetable fibre rope). It is not particularly elastic and does not float. Despite its expense it is used in competitive yachting.

Most rope consists of three strands that are twisted together from yarn which is itself spun from thin fibres. The twisting process that forms rope is known as 'laying up'. However, some rope is prepared by braiding, whereby the cord has two distinct layers, an outer protective sheath and the inner core which provides the rope with its strength.

Braided rope is very flexible and can be used easily with equipment such as snap links. It is softer and easy to handle but some knots may not hold particularly well. Although less flexible, twisted rope is good for heavy work such as anchoring and mooring and tends to hold knots very well indeed. As all the rope is visible, signs of damage and wear can be easily identified, unlike braided rope where damage to the core might not be seen.

Fishing Lines

The most popular material used in fishing is monofilament, a single strand of nylon that is available in a wide variety of breaking strengths. Other materials used include Dacron, braided wire (coated and un-coated) and wire.

The nylon used in the composition of monofila-ment fibre is quite tough but can be affected by heat, ultraviolet rays from the sun or fluorescent lighting and prolonged exposure to salt water.

Basic Terms

There are three parts to a line which are considered when tying knots:

The End
The loose end of the rope; the working portion with which a knot is tied.

The Bight
The slack middle portion of the rope, the part on which the knot is tied.

The Standing Part
The main part of the line, the unused left-over section.

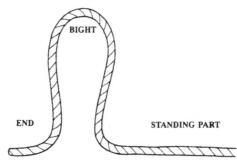

Loops

When the end is crossed over the bight, this forms an overhand loop.

When the end is crossed under the standing part, this forms an underhand loop.

Turn

Taking a turn involves carrying the loop around the standing part of the rope.

Basic Knots

The Overhand Knot

This is the smallest knot, used in the formation of many other knots and as a basic stopper knot, to prevent fraying at the end of a rope or string.

1 Form and overhand loop.
2 Take the end, push it upwards through the loop and draw it tight.

If it has been pulled tight, the Overhand Knot is very difficult to untie if the rope or cord is wet. It is therefore, impractical for use at sea.

The Multiple Overhand Knot

This is a very solid knot indeed.

1 Form an Overhand Knot as above but do not tighten it.

2 Draw the end through the loop as many times as you wish and pull it tight.

The Figure of Eight Knot

This is a more effective stopper knot than the Overhand Knot.

1 Form an overhand loop.

2 Take the end of the rope under the standing part to form an underhand loop (thus making the rope into the shape of an 8.

14

3 Then take the end and push it through the over-hand loop and draw it tight by pulling on both ends of the rope.

The Multiple Figure of Eight Knot

1 Form the first loop of the Figure of Eight Knot.
2 Cross the end under the standing part to form an underhand loop, followed by an overhand loop.
3 Repeat the process several times before passing the end through each of the loops at the top.
4 Draw on the end and the standing part and pull them tight to form the knot.

The Stevedore's Knot

1 Form an overhand loop and then pass the end underneath the standing part.

2 Pass the end through the original loop, as in a Figure of Eight Knot.

3 Take the end and turn it around the loop again and then draw it tight.

The Eye Knot

The Eye Knot can be used to create a strong loop to be secured around a post or a pole.

1 Form a bight in the middle of the rope.

2 Take both the standing parts to form an Overhand Knot, ensuring that a portion of the bight extends to form a loop.

3 Pull on the two standing parts of the rope to tighten the knot and form the appropriate size of loop.

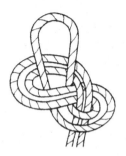

The Reef Knot

The Reef Knot or Square Knot is a classic sailor's knot, used to temporarily shorten a sail or create joints. The Reef Knot should be used on identical lines and should not be subject to significant strain, otherwise it may slip.

1 Take the end of the left-hand rope and turn it around the right-hand rope once.
2 Bend this end backwards so that it lies over the end of the right-hand rope to form a loop.

Basic Knots

3 Take up the end of the right-hand rope underneath and turn it around the left-hand end above so that both ends are doubled back over their standing parts.

4 Pull simultaneously on each end to fasten the knot.

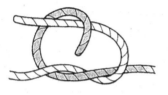 

The Granny Knot

This is very similar to the Reef Knot but it is not as strong and reliable and has a tendency to jam. Unlike the Reef Knot the Granny Knot does not lie flat when tightened.

1 Take the end of one rope and form an overhand turn around the end of the second rope.

2 Take up this end again and on this occasion form an underhand turn around the end of the second rope.

3 Pull on both ends to tighten the knot.

The Draw Knot

This is a Reef Knot with a bight formed in one end to enable a quick release.

1 Follow steps 1 and 2 for the Reef Knot.

2 Form a bight in the end of the right-hand rope and fold this over the left-hand end.

3 Pull on the bight and the left-hand end to tighten the formation.

The Bow Knot

This knot is useful in situations where it is necessary for the knot to be undone quickly.

1 Form a loose Overhand Knot and form a bight in the standing part of the rope.

2 Take the end over the bight and around it to form a second knot.

The Slip Knot

The Slip Knot is a familiar formation which is easy to tie and can be quickly released by pulling on the end.

1 Hold the end in the left hand and form an overhand loop in the standing part with the right hand.

2 Draw the standing part upwards through the loop to form a bight.

3 Hold the bight and tighten the knot by pulling the end.

The Double Slip Knot

1 Form an overhand loop.

2 Form two bights on either side by drawing the right-hand standing part up and over the right-hand side of the loop and the left-hand standing part down and under the left-hand side of the loop.

3 Pull on both bights with equal tension to tighten the knot.

The Double Slip Knot is easily released by pulling on both standing parts of the rope.

Hitches

Hitches are used for fixing rope to an object. Sailors, for example, will use hitches to moor boats. They are designed to withstand significant traction and yet be easily undone. A hitch can be made around a particular object, for example a ring or a post, as opposed to a loop which will be formed first and then placed over the object.

The Clove Hitch
This hitch is commonly used by sailors, campers and climbers, all of whom have different names for it and use it in different formations.
1 Take the end of the rope and wind it once anti-clockwise around the post, ensuring that the end lies below the standing part.
2 Take the end and pass it around the post in the same way but on this occasion cross it above the first turn.
3 Tuck the end under the second turn.
4 Pull on the end and the standing part to tighten the hitch.

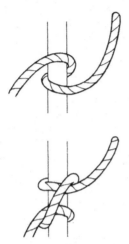

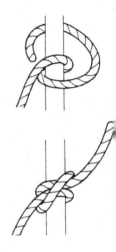

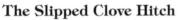

The Slipped Clove Hitch

This is particularly useful if the hitch needs to be untied when the rope is under strain. This involves creating a bight on the second turn and pulling the bight through it. This leaves the end exposed, to be pulled to quickly release the knot.

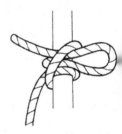

Clove Hitch for a Rope under Strain

This method is used by sailors for mooring craft to a bollard, a short metal post on a quayside or on the deck of a ship.

1 Take hold of the rope and draw it quickly towards you. Form a loop around the bollard.
2 Take hold of the slack end of rope below the bollard and form a second loop and then drop this over the bollard.
3 Hold onto the end and hitch will tighten itself from the strain exerted on the rope.

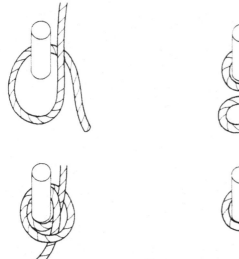
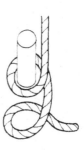

The Half Hitch

The Half Hitch is very versatile, it is used in a wide variety of situations and as part of many other formations. However, it will not withstand much strain and should be used only as a temporary fastening.

1 Pass the end around the post in a clockwise direction.

2 Turn the around the standing part in an anticlockwise direction.

3 Tuck the end between the rope and the post.

4 Pull it tight to create a jam.

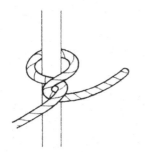 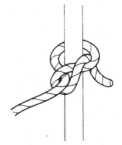

The Timber Hitch

This is basically a Half Hitch with an added turn between the rope and the post to create more of a jam.

26

1 Form a Half Hitch but do not pull it tight.
2 Turn the end around the rope and pull down on it once more before tightening.

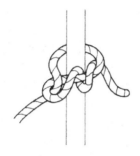

The Crossing Hitch
This simple hitch will be familiar to anyone who has tied a package.

1 Pass the end once around the object and underneath the standing part.
2 Draw the end upwards and backwards while drawing the standing part in the opposite direction.
3 To create a jam pass the end once around the object, tuck

it in between the rope and the object and pull on the standing part to tighten the hitch.

Again this hitch is useful as a temporary measure but will not withstand much strain.

The Fisherman's Bend

Also known as the Anchor Bend, this is a particularly strong hitch.

1 Take the end and pass it around the post (or over a ring) twice.

2 Pass the end around the standing part and draw it underneath both turns.

3 The end should then be passed around the standing part again and pulled tight between the rope and the standing part.

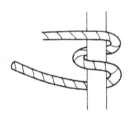

 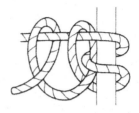

The Rolling Hitch

This is commonly used by climbers and sailors for affixing lighter rope to a heavy rope with tension on it.

1 Turn the end of the working rope twice around the heavier rope.

2 Draw it across and above the standing part to form a Half Hitch around the heavier rope, so that the end is parallel to the standing part.

3 To tighten the hitch, the standing part should be pulled downwards.

The Slipped Rolling Hitch

The Slipped Rolling Hitch is much easier to undo and can be made by forming a bight before making the final Half Hitch around the heavier rope. This leaves the end free on the opposite side to be pulled to release the hitch.

The Cow Hitch

As the name suggests this hitch is frequently used to tether cattle to a ring or a post, but is also used for temporarily affixing baggage labels and keys.

1 Pass the end through the ring from front to back.
2 Pass the end in front of the standing part and draw it through the ring again, but on this occasion pass it from back to front.
3 Draw the end through the loop underneath, so that it sits parallel to the standing part which should be pulled to tighten it.

The Cow Hitch should be used as a temporary fastening only.

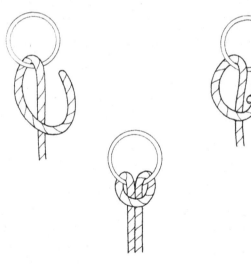

The Pile Hitch
This hitch is ideal for using with a post.
1 Make a bight in the middle of the rope or leave a long end.
2 Hold the bight against the post and turn the working part around the post and above the bight in an anticlockwise direction.
3 Take up the bight and pull it over the post. Pull on the standing parts of the rope to tighten the hitch.

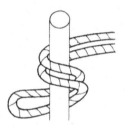

The Double Pile Hitch
This simply involves making a second turn around the post before feeding the bight over the top of the post.

The Halter Hitch

This hitch is both easy to form and simple to release.

1 Take the end around the post and form an under-hand loop opposite the standing part.
2 Pass the end underneath the standing part and then draw it around the rope.
3 Form a bight in the end and then feed the bight through the loop.
4 Pull gently on the standing part to tighten the hitch.

The Clara Hitch

This is ideal for joining a lightweight line to the end of a larger diameter rope.

1 Allow a long end in the lighter (working) rope and

pass it twice around the end of the thicker rope.
2 Turn the end back over the standing part and then tuck it under the first turn.
3 Pull on the standing part and the end to tighten the formation.

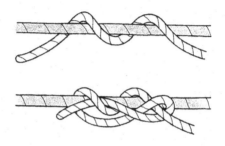

The Midshipman's Hitch

This hitch can be formed around a post or can be formed before being put around an object, and adjusted thereafter to ensure adequate tightness.

1 Form a Half Hitch followed by another Half Hitch.

2 Turn the end around the standing part once more.
3 Draw it through the loop to tighten it.

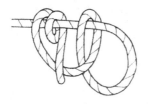

The Cat's Paw

This is commonly used for hitching rope to a hook.

1 The rope should be formed into two equal standing parts with a bight formed at the top.
2 Take the bight and fold it under the two standing
   parts to form two loops.
3 Twist these loops up to four times in opposite
   directions (clockwise for the left-hand loop and
   anticlockwise for the right-hand loop).
4 Pass both these loops over the hook and pull on
   the standing parts to tighten the hitch.

The Bill Hitch

This hitch is also used for tying rope to a hook and is particularly useful when a rope has to be tied and released quite rapidly.

1. Take the end of the rope and feed it through the mouth of the hook from behind.
2. Pass the end around the top of the hook and then pull it forward over the point of the hook.
3. Finally feed it through the loop of the rope and pull on the standing part to tighten the hitch.

The Draw Hitch

This hitch is formed with a bight to allow quick and easy release, so it is useful for making temporary fastenings. However, it will also withstand a certain amount of tension and climbers find it useful for lowering objects.

1 Form a bight by folding the long end back against the standing part and hold it at the neck.

2 Feed the bight over the pole (working from back to front) and then reach through the middle of the bight to take the standing part and pull it through, forming a second bight which should be pulled upwards.

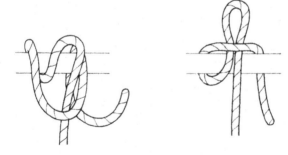

3 Holding this tight, take the end and a form a third bight and feed this up through the loop that has been formed above the post.

4 To tighten the hitch, hold the last bight while pulling on the standing part. This will then leave the end free to be pulled for a quick release.

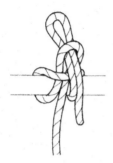 

The Slippery Hitch

This is made by forming a Slip Knot in the working part of the rope (i.e. nearer to the end as opposed to the standing part). An Overhand Knot is then formed in the end of the rope and can be repeated two or three times to establish a bigger knot. The advantage in this is that the Overhand Knot will prevent the Slip Knot from unravelling when the loop is placed over a post.

The Ground Line Hitch

Originally used by deep-sea fishermen this hitch is now more commonly used for tethering.

1 Pass the end around the object once.
2 Pass the end across in front of the standing part in a clockwise direction and once around the object.
3 Take the end in front of this last turn and below the first in an anticlockwise direction.
4 Pull on the standing part and the end to tighten the formation.

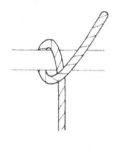
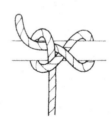

The Net Line Knot

This is similar to the Ground Line Hitch and was also used by fishermen.

1 Pass the end around the post.

2 Pass the end around the post and the standing part twice.

3 Draw the end across both these turns and tuck it beneath the first turn in an anticlockwise direction.

4 Tighten by pulling on the end and the standing part.

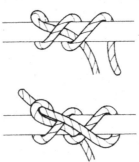

The Buntline Hitch

This involves forming two Half Hitches, the second of which is jammed by the first, thereby making this a very solid hitch to use.

1 Pass the end around the object once in an anti-clockwise direction and form a Half Hitch on the standing part.

2 Form a second Half Hitch below the first and tuck

the end through in between the rope and the first Half Hitch.

3 Pull on the end and the standing part to tighten the formation.

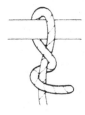 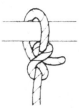

The Constrictor Knot

This is a highly versatile and simple knot that can make a temporary binding or be used for a host of practical purposes in the home. However, it does not hold on objects that have corners or flat planes and is, therefore, best used on objects which are cylindrical in shape or on sacking or pliable material.

1 Take the end of the rope and turn it twice anti-clockwise around the object, forming a half Overhand Knot with the second turn.

2 Take the end and tuck it underneath the first turn.

3 Pull on both ends to tighten the formation.

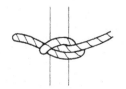 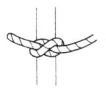

The Transom Knot

This is a practical knot for fixing smaller objects crosswise to a larger pole or piece of wood, for example in constructing a garden trellis.

1 Hold the object horizontally in position to the pole.

2 Take up the end and draw it up over the object, ensuring that the standing part lies over the object also.

3 Turn the end around the pole, back over the standing part and then down and around the pole again, below the object.

4 Draw the end upwards underneath both turns and pull on both the end and the standing part to tighten the formation.

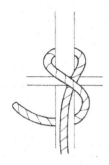

The Killick Hitch

This is basically a Timber Hitch followed with a Half Hitch and a few extra turns. It is appropriate for moving or hauling objects in an upright position.

1 Form a Half Hitch about two-thirds of the way up the object, so that the standing part extends upwards beyond the length and the end is drawn downwards, towards the base.

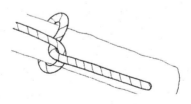

2 Form a Timber Hitch below the Half Hitch, about one-third of the way up the object. Turn the end around the standing part several times more before tightening the formation.

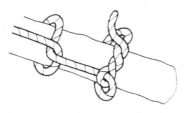

The Slip Knot with Half Hitch
This is very similar to the Slippery Hitch.

1 Form a Slip Knot.

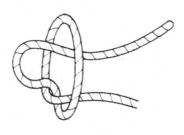

2 Form a Half Hitch around the standing part, below the Slip Knot, and pull on the loop and the standing part to complete the formation.

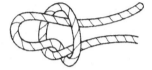

Bends

Bends are used to join two ropes together to form a longer rope, but they should always be regarded as a temporary measure—a more secure and permanent join can be made by splicing. Generally a bend should be formed using ropes of the same diameter and the same material, although there are a few exceptions to this rule.

The Sheet Bend

Also known as the Flag Bend, this versatile knot is ideal for tying ropes of different weight and thickness, joining the ends of a single rope or the ends of two identical ropes. The knot is easily released but jams effectively when strain is put on both the ropes.

1 Form a bight in the end of one rope and hold the bight firmly in position by holding the standing part against the end.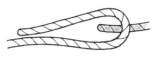

2 Take the end of the second rope and draw it up through the centre of the bight and turn it around the end and the standing part.

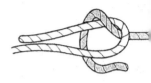

3 Tuck the end underneath its own standing part and pull on both ropes to tighten the formation.

The Double Sheet Bend

In doubling the knot the Sheet Bend formation becomes more secure.

1 Form the Sheet Bend as in steps 1–2 above.

2 Take two more turns around the end and the standing part before tucking the end in.

The Slipped Sheet Bend

This allows the knot to be released quickly, particularly when the rope is under strain. Form a Sheet Bend as before but form a bight in the end and pull this through the loop.

The Carrick Bend

The Carrick Bend is commonly used by climbers for joining two ropes and is a particularly good knot for heavy rope.

1 Form an overhand loop in the end of the rope and hold this firmly in position.

2 Take the second rope and pass it under the standing part, over the end and up through the centre of the loop in the first rope.

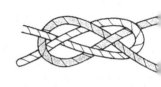

    Then pass this end over its own standing part and down through the loop to form a second overhand loop.

3 Pull on both the standing parts to tighten.

The Carrick Mark II

Although not strictly a Carrick Bend this formation is rather similar and can be used in the same way.

1 Lie the ends of the rope parallel to one another.

2 Take the end of the top rope and bend it backwards underneath its own standing part to form a loop.

3 Take the end of the bottom rope and bend it backwards passing it through the centre of the loop in the top rope and then draw it underneath its own standing part.

4 Take up the end of each rope and turn it over its own standing part and up through the loop of the opposing rope.

5 Pull on both ends to tighten the formation.

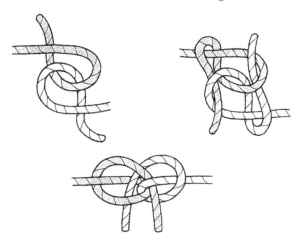

The Englishman's Knot

Known variously as the Fisherman's Knot, the Water Knot and the English Knot, this formation is ideal for joining relatively lightweight rope or angling lines. Although it is a simple knot to form it is very strong and reliable if used on the right kind of line.

1 Place the ends of the two ropes parallel to one another, allowing roughly 12 inches (approximately 30 cm) at the end of each rope for this.
2 Take up one rope and form an Overhand Knot around the second rope.
3 Repeat this with the second rope around the first.

Bends

4 Pull on both standing parts to secure the formation—the knot should have one end lying above the rope and one below if it has been formed correctly.

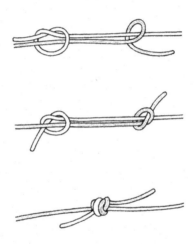

The Flemish Knot
This is simply a Figure of Eight Knot using two ropes.
1 Lie the ends of the ropes parallel to one another.
2 Form a Figure of Eight Knot with both ropes.

3 Draw on the standing parts of both tighten the knot.

The Surgeon's Knot
The Surgeon's Knot is strong and reliable but less bulky than other knots of this type.

1 Take up the ends of both ropes and turn the left-hand end twice around the right-hand rope.

Bends

2 Bring both ends to point upwards and again turn the left-hand end twice around the right-hand rope.

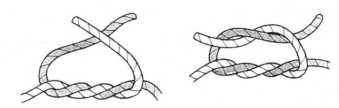

3 Hold both ends with their standing parts and draw them in opposite directions to tighten the knot.

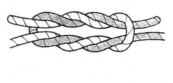

The Double Fisherman's Knot

This is frequently used by fishermen, campers and climbers on lighter rope.

1 Take the ropes and hold the ends parallel to and overlapping one another.
2 Take the end of one rope and turn it around the end of the second rope from front to back to form a Figure of Eight Knot
3 Insert the end into the left-hand loop of the knot and pull on the standing part to tighten it.

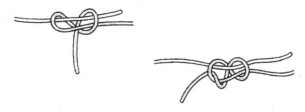

4 Repeat this with the second rope by forming a Figure of Eight Knot around the first rope in the same way.

5 Once both ends have been formed pull on both standing parts to draw them together.

The Hunter's Bend
A relatively new knot, the Hunter's Bend is strong and reliable but can be easily released.
1 Take the end of one rope and form an Overhand Knot without tightening it.
2 Take up the second rope and draw the end through the centre of the loop in the Overhand Knot and back under its own standing part.

3 Bring this end up through the upper loop of the Overhand Knot and then down through its own loop.

4 Pull on the ends of both ropes gently to draw them slightly clear of the knots. Then pull on both standing parts to form the knot.

The Weaver's Knot

This is a variation of the Sheet Bend and is best used on string or a lightweight line.

1 Hold one rope horizontally and draw the end of the second rope upwards behind the end of the first.

2 Make an overhand loop with the second rope by passing the standing part behind its own end and back down in front of the first rope.

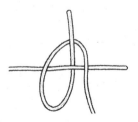

3 Now take up the end of the first rope, bend it backwards and pass it through the centre of this loop.
4 Pull gently on both standing parts to secure the knot.

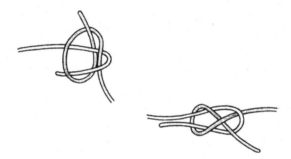

The Thief Knot

This looks very similar to the Reef Knot but is formed in a different way.

1 Form a bight in the end of one rope.
2 Insert the end of the second rope up through the centre of the bight and turn it around the end and the standing part.

3 Draw the end back through the centre of the bight so that it runs parallel with its own standing part.
4 Draw on the standing parts of both ropes to form the knot.

The Strap Knot

This is specifically devised for flat material such as a belt, a strap or webbing. It will not hold in rope or any other type of cordage.

1 Take hold of the ends of both straps and lie them parallel to one another but facing in opposite directions.
2 Take the end of the bottom strap and form a Half Hitch around the standing part of the top strap.

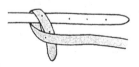

3 Take the end of the top strap and form a Half Hitch around the standing parts of the bottom strap.

4 Pull on the standing part of both straps to tighten the formation.

The Double Harness Bend

1 Lay the ends of the ropes overlapping and parallel to one another.

2 Take up the end of the top rope and turn it once around the standing part of the bottom rope and then tuck it under its own standing part.

3 Take up the end of the bottom rope and turn it once around the standing part of the top rope and then tuck it under its own standing part.

4 Take up the end of the top rope, turn it around its own standing part and draw it under the standing part of the bottom rope. Repeat this with the bottom rope around the top rope.

5 Pull with equal tension on the standing parts of both ropes to tighten the formation.

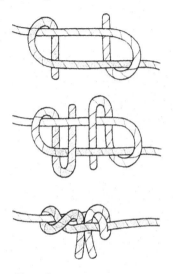

The Strait Bend
1 Take up the end of one rope and form an underhand loop.
2 Take the end of the second rope and draw this up through the first loop before taking it under its own standing part to form a second underhand loop. Ensure that there is a central loop left in between the two interlinking loops.

3 Take up both ends and pass them down through the central loop and pull on them to complete the formation.

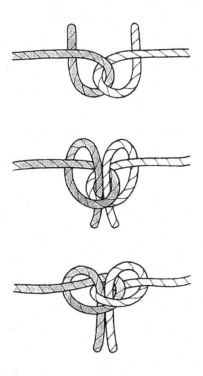

Loops

Unlike hitches loops are made on a rope before it is fixed to an object. The end is folded back along the standing part and a loop formed before a knot is completed to fix the formation.

The Bowline

1 Form an overhand loop in the standing part of the rope, then form a second large loop before pulling the end up through the first loop.
2 Pass the end behind and around the standing part inserting it back down through the smaller loop.
3 Hold the end against the adjacent part of the loop and with the other hand hold the rope. Pull with both hands to secure the formation.

The Slipped Bowline

This is easier to untie if the rope is subjected to great strain. Ensure that in forming the bowline you have enough rope at the end to be able to form a bight and pass this through the smaller loop.

The Improved Bowline

1 Begin to form the loop by following Step 1 of the method given for the Bowline.

2 Pull the end up through the smaller loop and behind the standing part. Then turn it once around
the standing part, from left to right, and then
down in front and through the smaller loop before
tightening it.

The Simple Noose

1 Turn the end of the rope around the standing part
in an overhand loop to form a bight.

2 Complete the turn with an Overhand Knot.
3 Pull on the end to tighten the formation.

The Hangman's Knot

1 Form a bight in the end of the rope, allowing a long end.
2 Form a second bight to lie opposite to the first.
3 Take up the end and make several turns about both bights working from right to left (an odd number of turns should be made).

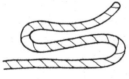

The right-hand bight will be left intact while the left-hand bight should be covered by most of the turns.

4 Draw the end through what remains of the left-hand loop to tighten the noose. The larger loop should run freely.

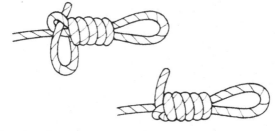

The Angler's Loop

Ideal for fine lightweight lines, this is a strong, reliable loop but it can be difficult to release. It is, therefore, used mainly for recreational purposes, such as angling and camping.

1 Form an underhand loop, passing the end anti-clockwise under the standing part.

2 Hold the neck of the loop and take the end around in front of the standing part and back behind the loop. This will form a second loop which should be kept slack.

Loops

3 Take the end and make a turn around the neck in front of the bight.

4 Take up the second loop and pass this up through the first bight.

5 Tighten the formation by holding the loop in position and pulling on the standing part.

The Spanish Bowline

1 Form a bight in the centre of the rope, cross the standing parts and double the bight back under the two strands to form a large loop.

2 Draw each strand upwards through the loop to form two bights at the top and twist these bights in an outward direction.

3 Take up the two sides of the original loop and draw them through the two top bights, working them over and then under.

4 Gently draw on the loops to tighten the knot at the centre.

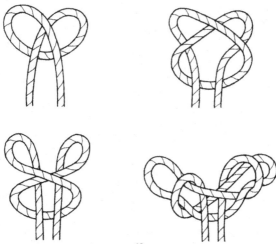

Loops

The Lasso

The loop of the lasso can be adjusted to the desired size as the knot can run freely along the rope.

1 Make a stopper in the end of the rope by forming an Overhand Knot.
2 Form a second Overhand Knot, without tightening it, and pass the end and the first knot back through the lower loop.
3 Take up the standing part and form a bight which should be drawn through the larger loop.
4 Pull on the bight and on the end to tighten the knot.

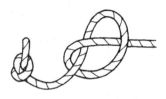

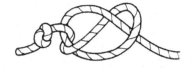

The Figure of Eight Bowline

1 Form a Figure of Eight Knot by taking the end up to form an overhand loop and then turn the rope

behind the standing part, forming a second (underhand) loop.

2 Bring the end down and feed it through the lower loop from front to back, then bring it to the front of this loop and feed it through again to create yet another loop.

3 Hold onto this last loop and carefully pull the knot tight to complete the formation.

The Figure of Eight Bowline will not withstand a great amount of strain.

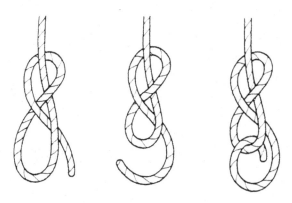

The Portuguese Bowline

The Portuguese Bowline is particularly good for holding and suspending heavy objects or for supporting somebody who is working in a position in which they are being suspended. It can be formed with more than two loops if desired. The greater the number of loops the greater the strength of the formation.

1 Make an overhand loop in the standing part of the rope and leave a long end.

2 Pass the end through this loop to form a second large loop and then repeat this to form another parallel loop of the same size.

3 Pass the end through the smaller loop, around the standing part and down again through the smaller loop.

4 Pull on the standing parts while holding the end against the larger loops.

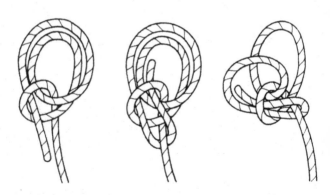

The Running Bowline

This knot is frequently used by sailors because it slides easily but remains strong and reliable: it is also easily undone.

1 Take up the end of the rope and form a large underhand loop.
2 Hold the top left-hand corner of this loop and twist it outwards (this will make the whole formation resemble the symbol &).
3 Pass the end through this small loop from back to front, then turn it around the rope below and back up through the loop.
4 Tighten the formation by pulling the end and the left-hand side of the large loop.

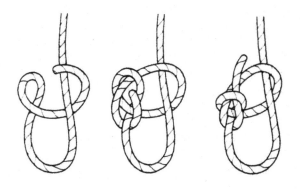

Loops

The Bowline on a Bight

This is ideal for use when the ends of the rope are not accessible. Like the straightforward Bowline it is commonly used at sea and is frequently used in rescue situations.

1 Form a bight in the centre of the rope.
2 Make an overhand turn with the bight around the standing parts and feed the bight through the turn; this will form a second loop.
3 Take the bight and fold it back over and behind both loops.
4 The lower loop will now be the larger of the two and this should be adjusted to the desired size.

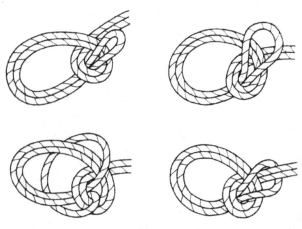

The Tarbuck Knot

This knot has been developed to withstand heavy and sudden loading, but is easy to untie. It is ideal for use on a ring.

1 Pass the end through the ring from behind and turn it around the standing part three times in a clockwise direction, working from bottom to top.
2 Turn the end around the standing part and up through the loop.
3 Pull on the standing part and the end to tighten the knot.

The Three Part Crown

This knot is frequently used by campers for hanging equipment. Although it can withstand heavy strain it can prove difficult to untie if heavy objects are suspended for a long time.

Loops

1 Form a bight in the centre of the rope and hold it in place by pinching it at the neck.
2 Push down the centre of the bight to form two equal loops. Take the standing parts upwards in an anticlockwise direction to lie across the neck of the right-hand loop. This will form a third loop.
3 Take the right-hand loop and fold it down across the standing parts.

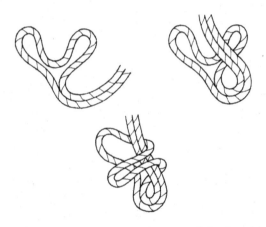

4 Fold the left-hand loop over the right-hand loop and then pass it through the loop at the base.
5 To tighten the knot pull on the right- and left-hand loops, taking care that they are of equal size.

The True Lover's Knot

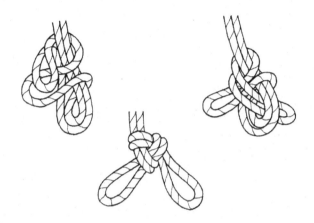

The True Lover's Knot

This is now generally used as a decorative knot but it can be used as a fancy line on smaller items such as a penknife or a whistle.

1 Leaving a long end, form an Overhand Knot without tightening it and hold this upright in the left hand.

2 Form a second loose knot to sit opposite the first knot.

77

Loops

3 Pull on the portion of rope between the two knots to form a bight at the top.

4 Using the index and middle finger on each hand, reach through the turns on the knots at the side and take hold of the rope where it is intertwined at the centre of the formation.

5 Draw these out through the loops at the side.

6 When tightening the knot ensure that the all three loops are of equal size.

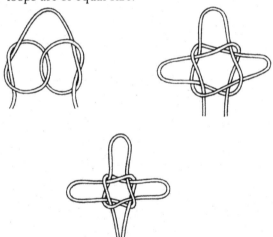

The Artillery Loop

As the name suggests, this loop was once used by soldiers to fasten a pull to artillery equipment such as cannons. Made in heavy, large diameter rope it is now sometimes used by climbers.

1 Take up the end of the rope and form a large underhand loop. Leave the end lying in a downwards direction across the left-hand portion of the loop.

2 Take hold of the bottom of the loop and twist it anticlockwise to make a second loop.

3 Hold this loop tightly at the neck and pass it upwards between the end and the left-hand part of the loop.

4 Pull on the end and the standing part to complete the formation.

Loops

The Fisherman's Loop
This is probably best used as a temporary loop which
will not be subjected to much weight or strain as it
has a low breaking strength.

1 Take up the end and form an overhand loop.
2 Bring the end back in front of the standing part
and form a second underhand loop.

3 Take up the part of the bight at the top of the
formation and pass it up through the loop from
underneath (i.e. the small loop created by the
overlapping loops).

4 Hold the end and the standing part together in one hand and pull on the bight to tighten the formation.

Shortening Formations

On occasions it is possible that you might find yourself with too much rope—the obvious answer might seem to be to cut it to the right length, but this will result in limiting the use and value of an expensive piece of rope. By using various formations it is possible to temporarily shorten the rope and even to increase the usage of a rope by getting rid of portions that have become worn or damaged in some way.

The Sheepshank

This is synonymous with seafaring. For centuries sailors have favoured this knot because it is easily released and does not create wear on the rope.

1 Form a double bight in the rope to resemble the letter 'S'.
2 Take up the right-hand standing part and twist it to form a small underhand loop. Feed this loop over the adjacent bight
3 Take the left-hand standing part, form a loop in the same way and feed this over the other bight.
4 Pull with equal tension on each side of the rope to secure the knot.

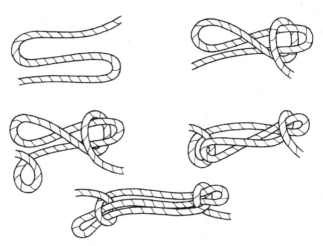

The Catshank

This formation is similar to the Sheepshank and it can also be made without using the ends of the rope.

1 Form two Slip Knots in the rope, at least 12 inches (approximately 30 cm) apart.
2 Form two bights in the rope between the knots by doubling up the rope.
3 Draw each bight through the loops in the opposing knots.
4 To tighten, pull with equal tension on the rope on either side of the knots.

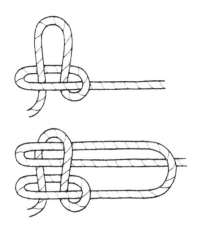

The Dogshank

This is a very simple shortening formation which can be used where both ends are accessible.

1 Form a double bight to resemble the letter 'S'.
2 Take the end and tie it in an Overhand Knot around the bulge of the opposite bight.
3 Repeat the process with the end on the opposing bight.

The Monkey Chain

This can also be used as decorative lanyard knot.

1 Allow a long end, depending on how much you need to shorten the rope by.
2 Form a Slip Knot around the end, without tightening it.
3 Take up the standing part and form a bight feeding it through the bight which is lying below the Slip Knot. Ensure that these bights are of equal size.
4 Continue to form bights in this way until a chain has been formed.
5 Turn the end through the final bight and its own loop and pull on both ends to tighten the chain.

The Double Chain Twist

This may appear a little complicated but the principle is similar to plaiting with a three strand cord.

1 Form two bights in the rope to resemble the letter 'M'. The end should sit on the left and the standing part on the right.
2 Take up the part of the rope between the two bights and twist it anticlockwise to form an overhand loop. The end and the two parts of this loop will be the working parts.

3 Take the end, insert it into the centre of the loop and pull the end clear.
4 Take up the left-hand part of the loop and cross it over the right-hand part.
5 Take up the right-hand part and cross it over the end.
6 Continue in this way always ensuring that the end is drawn clear of the whole formation.

7 Once the rope has been sufficiently shortened, push the end through the last bight on the chain and pull on both the ends to tighten the formation.

Overhand Knot with Sheepshank

This can be used when both ends of the rope are easily accessible.

1 Take up the centre of the rope and form a double bight.
2 Tie the bights in an Overhand Knot, pulling on them to tighten the knot.
3 Form a Half Hitch around each loop with the adjacent rope and pull the ends through the loops.
4 Pull on the ends to tighten the knot.

The Loop Knot

This knot is very straightforward and proves its value when used to eliminate a worn section of rope.

1 Make a bight in the centre of the rope or the point at which the rope has become worn.
2 Form an overhand knot with the bight around the to standing parts.

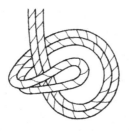

Shortening Formations

3 Hold the standing parts and pull on the bight to tighten the formation.

Stopper Knots

Traditionally, stopper knots were used to prevent a rope from running out through a hole or through a block. However, they can now be regarded as knots that are both decorative and functional.

The Crown Knot
This stopper knot is used as the basis for other knots but never on its own.
1 Unlay the rope into short strands and seal the ends by heating or whipping them.
2 Take up one of the strands and form a bight in it.

 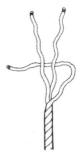

3 Take up the strand next to it and pass it down through the bight, forming a second bight.

4 Take up the last strand and pass this down through the second bight, forming a third bight.

5 Then take up the first strand again and pass it down through the third bight.

6 Carefully pull on the strands to manipulate the knot.

The Wall Knot

This is similar to the Crown Knot with the difference that the each strand is pulled upwards through the bight next to it as opposed to downwards, as with the Crown Knot. Once the knot has been formed the strands are layed up again, whipped and the ends trimmed.

The Back Splice

This is a hybrid of stopper knot and a splice whereby a Crown Knot is formed and the remaining length of unravelled strands are then tucked back into the strands of the rope, against the lay.

The Diamond Knot

This is very similar to the Wall Knot but in this case the strands are passed up through the bight of the next but one strand. Once the knot has been formed the ends are then layed up, whipped at the top and the ends trimmed.

The Matthew Walker Knot

1 Form a Wall Knot but do not work it down to tighten it.
2 Pass each strand up through the next bight once more and then work the strands to tighten the formatic⁻

Angling Knots

The Bimini Twist

This is regarded as one of the most important fishing knots to learn and is the basis of many knot-tying formations.

1 Measure about 6 feet (1.8 metres) of line and double it up, holding the end and the standing part together in your right hand.

2 Insert your left hand into the bight at the centre of the line and twist the loop 20 times to form 20 twists in the line.

3 Holding firmly onto the end and the standing part, slip the loop over your feet and knees to extend the size of the loop and tighten the twists on the line.

4 At the same time hold the end and the standing part at an angle of about 45° each to the line. This will tighten the twists, evenly without allowing them to become entangled.

5 Move the standing part back to its upright vertical position and the end to a 90° angle to the line. This will cause the end to jump over the first twist in the line.

6 Gradually spread your knees apart to allow the end to roll over the twists in parallel coils.

7 Maintain the tension and hold the point at which the last roll covers the twists.

8 Form a Half Hitch with the end over one side of the loop and tighten it by pulling the end towards you.

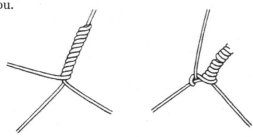

9 Turn the end around both standing parts of the loop and form a Half Hitch without tightening it. Then turn it twice more around the standing parts of the loop.

10 Pull gently on the end to tighten the knot up against the rolled section of the line.

11 Trim the end to within about ⅛ inch (approximately 7mm) of the knot to complete the formation.

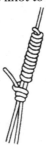

The Crawford Knot

Ideal for tying a nylon line to an eyed hook or a swivel, this is a strong, easily tied knot.

1 Draw the end of the line through the eye of the hook, leaving an allowance of 8 inches (approximately 20 cm) for tying off the knot.

2 Pass the end behind the standing part, forming a loop.

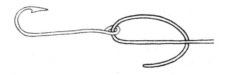

3 Take the end down and around the loop and then draw it upwards in front of the loop, as in a figure of eight formation.

4 Insert the end between the top of the loop and the standing part and then draw on the standing part to tighten the knot at the base of the hook.

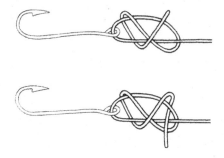

The Blood Knot

Also known as the Barrel Knot, this knot is used for joining two lines together.

1 Place the ends parallel to one another, allowing about 6 inches (approximately 15 cm) for each end.

2 Take up the end of the left-hand line and turn it twice around the end of the right-hand line.

3 Bend this end back under the point at which the lines first cross and then pass it upwards.

4 Take up the end on the right-hand side and turn this twice around the left-hand rope before bending it backwards and down through the same point.

5 Draw the formation tight by pulling first on the ends and then on the standing points with equal tension. If properly formed one end should lie horizontally above the knot and one below.

The Improved Clinch Knot

This is an ideal knot for tying into an eyed hook or a swivel ring.

1 Insert the end of the line through the eye, leaving approximately 6–8 inches (approximately 15–20 cm) for tying off the knot.

2 Hold the hook in the left hand and with the right hand make five turns around the standing part with the end, holding the line taut.

3 Without releasing the turns, relax the tension on the line and insert the end through the loop which has been formed between the eye and the first turn. This will form a second loop.

4 Draw the end through this second loop and pull on it to complete the knot.

The Jansik Special
This knot is particularly good for tying light monofilament line onto a swivel or an eyed hook.

1 Draw the end through the eye or ring, leaving around 12 inches (approximately 30 cm) to tie off the knot.

2 Bring the end around and again draw it through the eye to form a loop.

3 Pinch the loop to hold it in place, take the end around and insert it once more through the eye of the hook to form two complete parallel loops. Hold the standing part against the loops.

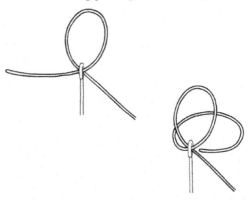

4 Bring the end close to the eye and turn it three times around the loops and the standing part.

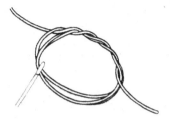

5 To complete the knot it is necessary to pull on the end, the standing part and the hook. This is best achieved by holding the end between your teeth and the hook and the standing part in your hands. Trim off any excess end off.

The Branch Knot

This can be used for joining several short lines to one longer line, for example when attaching several hooks to one line at regular intervals.

1 Take up the end of the shorter line and turn it around the main line to form a large overhand loop.

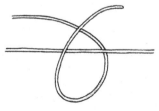

2 Turn the end through the loop and around the line several times, ensuring that these turns do not overlap.

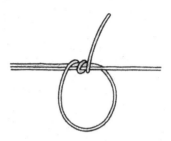

3 Gently pull on the end and the standing part, pulling the original large loop tight.

The Blood Bight
1 Form a bight leaving a long end. Hold the end and the standing part together.
2 Take hold of the bight, fold it back and turn it once

around the end and the standing part, thereby forming another loop.

3 Take the bight and pass it up through the loop and pull to tighten the formation.

The Perfection Loop

1 Take the end around the standing part to form an overhand loop.
2 Form a bight at the side and pass the end back through the centre of the overhand loop.

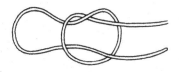

3 Pass the end under the standing part and then pass it through the point at which the standing part first crosses with the overhand loop at the top.

4 Pull with equal tension on the standing part and the end to tighten the formation.

The Quadruple Fisherman's Knot
This is basically the Double Fisherman's Knot with an extra turn.

1 Overlap the ends of both ropes and hold them parallel to one another, with the right-hand rope lying above the left.

2 Take the end of the right-hand rope and form a Figure of Eight Knot, working from left to right. Then turn the end twice more around the rope.

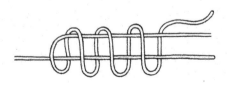

3 Take the end and draw it through all the loops.

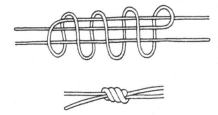

4 Repeat this process with the end of the second rope.
5 When both knots have been formed, pull on the standing parts of both ropes to tighten the formation.

The Turtle Knot

This knot creates a strong pull for a curved hook.
1 Pass the end of the line up through the eye of the hook.
2 Form a loose Slip Knot, folding the end back over the standing part and leaving a loop.

3 Take the point of the hook up through the centre of the loop.

4 Pull on the standing part and the end of the rope to tighten the knot.

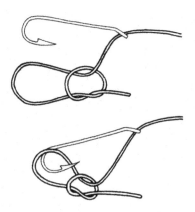

The Double Turle Knot

This is simply a Turle Knot with an extra turn that provides extra strength.

1 Pass the end down through the eye and turn it back under the standing part to form a loop.

2 Form a second loop in the same way and hold both loops parallel against the standing part.

3 Draw the eye of the hook through the two loops

and take the end around the standing part and under the shank.

4 Tie a Slip Knot to complete the formation.

The Improved Turle Knot

This knot lacks the strength of the basic Turle Knot but it is particularly useful for maintaining a straight pull when a fly is tied to a hook.

1 Pass the end down through the eye of the hook and turn it around the standing part to form a loop.

2 Pass the end through the loop three times to create a smaller loop before forming a Slip Knot.

3 Hold the end and pull on the larger loop to tighten the formation.

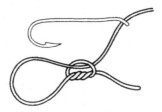

4 Pass the large loop over the hook (and the fly if attached) and pass the end through the loop once more.

5 Complete the formation by pulling gently on the standing part and trim off any excess end.

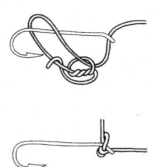

The Dropper Loop

1 Form a loop in the line and use one part of the line to create an unequal number of turns around the loop (5–7 for example).
2 Form a bight in the bottom of the loop and feed this through the space at the central turn.
3 Pull on the bight and both parts of the rope with equal tension to tighten the formation.

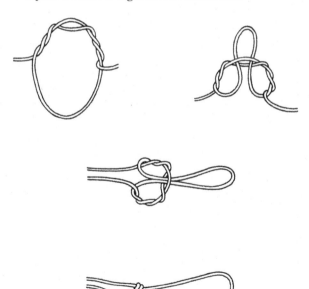

The Hook Tie

This is a basic strong knot for tying an eyed hook to a line.

1 Pass the end up through the eye of the hook.

2 Turn the end once around the standing part from back to front and then turn the end around the loop and the standing part from front to back.

3 Pass the end around the back and then through the centre of the first loop and pull to tighten it.

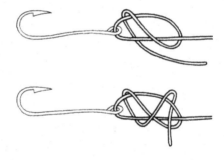

Methods of attaching a line to an eyed hook
Method 1

1 Pass the end down through the eye of the hook and turn it once around the standing part, forming an overhand loop.

2 Turn the end twice around the base of the loop.
3 Gently pull on the hook while holding the standing part to tighten the knot.

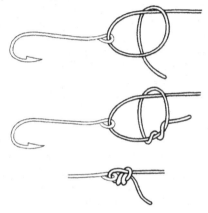

Method 2

1 Pass the end down through the eye of the hook
and once around the standing part to form a loop.
2 Pass the end around the base of the loop and then
turn it around the top to form a second loop in a
figure of eight formation.

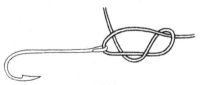

3 Pass the end through the centre of the first loop and turn it once around the base.

4 Pull gently on the hook and the standing part to tighten the formation.

Method 3

1 Pass the end down through the eye of the hook and turn it around the shank to form a loop, working in an anticlockwise direction.

2 Take the end once around the standing part of the line and through the centre of the loop which is lying above the shank.

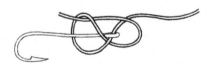

3 Pull on the standing part while holding the end to tighten the formation.

Method 4

1 Pass the end down through the eye of the hook and turn it once around the shank to form a loop, working in an anticlockwise direction.

2 Pass the end upwards in front of the standing part and turn it once around to form a second loop.

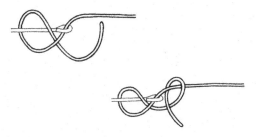

3 Take the end behind the standing part and tuck it between the standing part and the top of the loop.

4 Draw the end through the portion of the loop lying above the shank.

5 Tighten the formation by holding the end firmly against the shank and pulling on the standing part.

Method 5

1 Pass the end downwards through the eye of the hook.

2 Turn the end around the shank several times (about four turns should be sufficient).

3 Bend the end backwards and pass it back along the shank and down through the eye again.

4 Transfer the turns onto the standing part. The

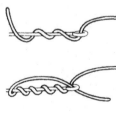

turn nearest to the eye should be the first turn on the standing part, the second on the shank should be passed over the first turn to sit behind it, and so on until all the turns have been transferred.

5 Gently pull on the hook and the standing part to tighten the knot.

Method 6

1 Pass the end upwards through the eye of the hook.
2 Form a loose Overhand Knot around the shank and then draw the end upwards between the line and the shank to form a second loop.

3 Take the end back through the top of the second
loop and hold it while pulling on the standing part
to tighten the formation.

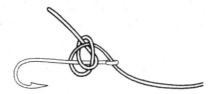

Knots for Flat Hooks
Flatted hooks are now rarely used in fishing, however, the following methods can be used to attach
such a hook to a line.

Method 1
1 Draw the end along under the shank of the hook.
2 Fold the end back and turn it once around the
shank and the adjacent standing part.
3 Repeat the turns around the shank and the standing part two or three times more.

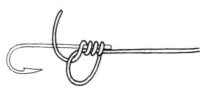

4 Bend the end backwards and pass it through the turns.

5 Pull on the end and the standing part to complete the formation.

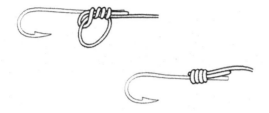

Method 2

1 Draw the end along the length of the shank.

2 Bend the end backwards and turn it once around the shank, leaving a bight.

3 Turn the end around the bight and the shank three or four times more, working from right to left.

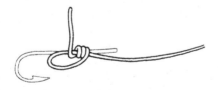

4 Pass the end down through the eye of the bight and pull gently on the standing part to tighten the formation.

Method 3

1 Draw the end along the top of shank of the hook.
2 Bend the end backwards and turn it around the shank and the standing part, leaving a bight. Repeat these turns up to three times, working from right to left.

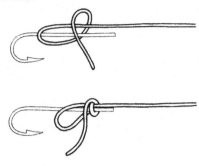

3 Pass the end down through the eye of the bight and tighten the formation by pulling gently on the end and then on the standing part.

Method 4
1 Form an overhand loop with two turns.
2 Form a figure of eight formation by pulling on the end and the standing part simultaneously.

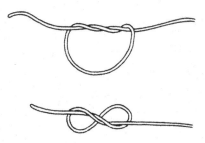

3 Pass the figure of eight formation onto the shank of the hook by passing the shank through the loops. The end should sit above the shank and the standing part below.

4 Pull on the end and the standing part to tighten the knot.

FASTENINGS FOR SWIVEL RINGS

Once a fish has taken up a baited line its movements can cause tangling in the line. Using a swivel ring enables the line to remain free from tangling.

The Double Stevedore Knot

1 Take up the end and pass it twice through the swivel ring.
2 Turn the end around the standing part several times, working from left to right
3 Pass the end through loops below the swivel ring and pull on it to tighten the formation.

The Cat's Paw (Anglers')

This is tied differently to the method described on page 35.

1 Form a bight in the centre of the line.
2 Pass the bight through the ring from back to front and then pass the standing parts through the centre of the bight.
3 Take each standing part and twist it around the adjacent side of the bight several times.
4 Pull on the standing parts to complete the formation.

Swivel Hitches

Method 1
This is an easy and strong knot to form.

1 Take up the end and pass it through the ring two or three times, ensuring that the turns do not become entangled.

2 Form a loose Overhand Knot around the standing part and then pull on the standing part and the end to complete the knot.

3 Repeat this with a line on the opposite ring. More strength can be provided by making extra turns on the Overhand Knot.

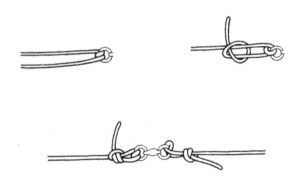

Method 2

This method enables the line to be tightened and fitted right into the ring.

1 Pass the end through the ring and turn it back once around its standing part to form an overhand turn.
2 Make several turns in this way, working from left to right, and then tuck the end through the bight sitting just behind the ring.
3 Pull on the swivel and the standing part to tighten the formation.
4 Repeat this with a line on the opposite ring.

Climbing Knots

Many of the knots previously covered are commonly used by climbers. For example, the Clove Hitch is frequently used for tying rope into the snaplink device known as a karabiner, while the bowline is used for tying into harnesses. Other knots have been devised specifically for emergency and self-rescue techniques or for ascending a rope.

This section has been devised to provide a general overview of the knots that are used in climbing activity and is not intended as a form of basic instruction. It is, of course, essential that anyone wishing to take up climbing should consult a fully-qualified climbing instructor to learn the proper techniques.

The Figure of Eight Knot

This is the most commonly-used basic knot for tying climbing rope into a harness or a belay anchor. It is easy to form, strong, versatile and relatively easy to release after loading. In addition to this, it is easy to identify if it has not been formed correctly—if it has not then it simply won't resemble a figure of eight.

The most common formation of the knot in climbing is illustrated below.

The Bowline

Formed as described on page 63, this is also commonly used in climbing for tying a rope into a harness, although it is not as popular as the Figure of Eight Knot as it tends to weaken the rope more. It is usually finished off with a half Double Fisherman's Knot to provide extra security.

The Clove Hitch (on a ring or karabiner)

The Clove Hitch is generally used in climbing for tying rope into a belay anchor. It should be noted that the Clove Hitch can be very difficult to undo if it has been formed in a rope that has sustained significant and sustained strain. In addition the hitch should not be formed in the end of a rope in case some slippage occurs.

1 Pass the end of the rope through the ring, working from back to front.
2 Pass the rope behind the standing part and through the ring again from behind.
3 Pass the rope through the loop that has been formed and pull on both standing parts to tighten the formation.

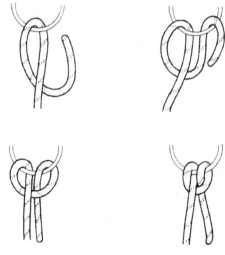

The Italian Hitch

Also known as the Munter Hitch or the Friction Hitch, this formation can be used on a locking karabiner for lowering and or as a direct belay. However, this hitch can twist and thus damage the rope quite badly.

1 Form a loop in the rope.
2 Take a strand of the rope across the main rope and run it parallel to the loop.
3 Insert the hitch into a locking karabiner.

The Ring Bend

Also known as the Tape Knot this is commonly used to complete a tape sling, which is a method of anchoring with climbing tape. This involves passing the completed loop of tape around the object to be used as an anchor.

1 Form an Overhand Knot in the end of one tape without tightening it.

2 Take up the other end of the second tape and trace the line through the first knot so that the end comes out on the opposite side.

3 Ensure that at least 2 inches (approximately 5 cm) of the ends is left free once the knot is formed.

4 Pull on both standing parts to tighten the knot, ensuring that the tape does not become twisted.

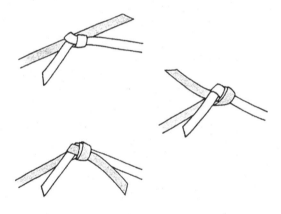

PRUSIK KNOTS

This is the collective name given to a series of knots which are commonly used by climbers for the ascent of a fixed rope, for temporarily securing a rope or for

lowering past a knot, among other uses. These slid-
ing friction knots work on the principle that a smaller diameter rope if wound around a thicker standing
rope will grip when loaded.

Generally a rope used for prusiking will be pre-
measured to the climber's individual requirement
and the ends will be tied off with a Double Fisherman's Knot, so that the working rope is already
formed into a loop. It is important that the Double
Fisherman's Knot is not included in the formation of
the Prusik Knot.

The Basic Prusik Knot

Used for ascending a rope, the Basic Prusik Knot
should be tied in a thinner cord around a large diameter rope. It is not ideal for use with ropes which
are wet or icy because on wet rope it jams easily and
on icy rope it may not grip. Once a load has been
taken on the rope the Prusik Knot cannot be untied
unless it is cut or unless the load has been removed.
It is, therefore, entirely inappropriate for use as a
safety back-up device or if subjected to a sudden and
intense loading strain.

The basic mechanism of the knot enables the
rope to slide but to tighten and seize if the load is
placed in on the prusik.

1 Form a bight in the centre of the working rope and hold it horizontally against the standing rope.

2 Take up both the standing parts of the working rope and pass them through the bight and turn them twice around the standing rope, working in a clockwise direction.

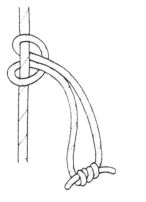
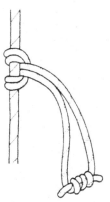

The Kieimheist Knot

The Kieimheist Knot can be tied in cord and in tape and is not so prone to jamming or slippage as the Basic Prusik Knot.

1 Form a bight in the middle of the cord and hold it against the standing rope.

2 Hold both strands of the cord parallel against one

another and turn them around the rope ensuring that the ropes do not become twisted and that each turn lies below the one above.

3 After three turns take the strands of the cord and pass them up through centre of the bight that sits on top of the turns.

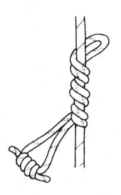 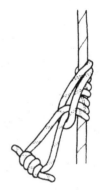

The French Prusik Knot

This knot can be used a safety back-up system or as an autobloc, a device that will lock around the rope and prevent slippage when subjected to any sudden loading but will also release easily, even when under a load. However, unlike many other Prusik Knots it is not recommended for use when ascending a rope.

1 Double the working rope and form a long bight

in the centre to which a snaplink will be attached. Hold the bight horizontally to the standing rope.

2 Take the two standing parts and hold them parallel. Wind them four times around the standing rope, working from top to bottom and from left to right.

3 Feed the bight and the opposite loop into the snaplink.

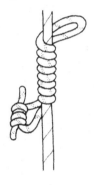 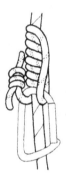

The Penberthy Knot

This knot does not jam and can be easily released. In addition it can also be tied using ropes of the same thickness and does not need a loop sling. However, both hands are required to tie the knot and its uses in climbing are fairly limited.

1 Turn the end of the working rope around the

standing rope five times working from top to bottom and from left to right.

2 Hold the standing part of the working rope in front of the standing rope and pass the end around it, again in an anticlockwise direction.

3 Turn the end around itself once or twice and insert it underneath one of these turns to secure the formation.

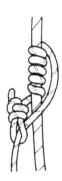

The Butterfly Knot
This is a good middleman's knot—it will not jam, it holds its shape and it can be pulled from any direction.

1 Allowing a long end, form a large overhand loop in the rope.

2 On the right-hand side of the loop, form a

second smaller loop by twisting the rope anti-clockwise.

3 Hold this loop at the neck and pass it over the point at which the rope crosses on the first loop. Continue to pass it under this point and up through the larger loop.

4 Pull on the smaller loop and the standing parts of the rope to tighten the knot.

The Guide Knot

This is simply a Figure of Eight knot made in the bight of the rope to form a safety knot.

1 Double the rope and form a bight large enough to fit around your waist and hold the standing parts together at this point, letting the bight drop.

2 Ensuring that the standing parts remain parallel, wind them around the bight twice, ensuring that you are left holding a loop.

Climbing Knots

3 Take hold of the bight and pass it through the centre of the loop and then pull with equal tension on the bight and the standing parts to complete the knot.

4 Check that the size of the bight is correct and adjust the knot accordingly.

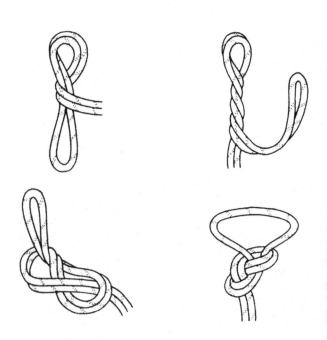

The Bachmann

1 Form a bight and clip this into a karabiner.
2 Hold the flat part of the karabiner (the 'back bar') against the standing rope and wind the working rope four times around the rope and the flat part of the snaplink.
3 Clip the end loop into the karabiner.

Decorative Knots

The Shamrock Knot

This ornamental knot is best formed on a short length of rope, since both ends are required. It is also easier to form the knot by laying the rope on a flat surface.

1 Form a loose Overhand Knot in the middle of the rope. Lay the knot at the bottom and place the ends of the rope to run upwards, either side of the loop.

2 Take the right-hand end and cross it under the loop towards the left-hand side.
3 Take up the left-hand end and cross it over the loop to lie on the right-hand side.

4 The end now lying on the left-hand side should be passed over the formation and down through the left-hand loop of the original Overhand Knot.

5 The end lying on the right-hand side should be passed under the formation and up through the right-hand loop of the Overhand Knot.

6 To tighten the formation pull gently on both ends while ensuring that the three loops are of similar size and are arranged in such a way that they a resemble the leaves of a shamrock.

The Oriental Knot

This is a simple example of the decorative oriental formations.

1 Form an overhand loop in the centre of the rope, an overhand loop to the left of this and an under-hand loop to the right.

Decorative Knots

2 Draw the ends downwards, to lie at the bottom of the formation and cross the right-hand end over the left.

3 Take up the end which now lies on the left-hand side and weave this upwards through the left-hand loop and centre top loop.

4 Take up the other end and weave this downwards through the right-hand loop and the centre top loop.

5 Gently draw the ends upwards to complete the formation.

The Japanese Bend

This knot necessitates the use of two ropes and is sometimes also used as the starting point for more complex decorative formations.

1 Take up one rope and form a bight in the end. Continue to maintain the form of the bight by holding it at the neck.

2 Take up the second rope and pass it in front of the neck of the bight, holding it in position at that point. Then draw the end through the centre of the bight, just below the neck, forming a second bight.

3 Continue to draw the end to make a third bight and then through the other side of the first bight.

4 Take up the end of the first rope and draw it

145

downwards over the second bight and through the centre of the third.

5 Alternately gently pull on the standing parts and the ends to form symmetrical knot.

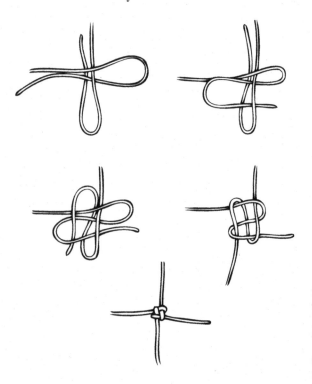

The Heaving Line Knot

Traditionally this was used to weight heaving lines
that were being thrown ashore or to another vessel. It
can also be used as a stopper knot or as a decorative
knot.

1 Form a long overhand loop in the rope and leave a
   long end.
2 Wind the end around the loop and the standing
   part of the rope in several turns, all of which
   should lie snugly beside one another. The number of turns made is a matter of individual choice,
   but a small loop must be left.

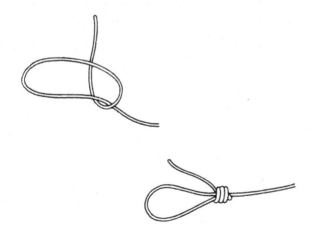

3 Once all the turns have been made pass the end of
the rope down through the small loop and pull on
the standing part to tighten the knot.

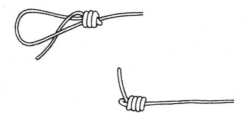

The Jury Mast Knot

As with the Heaving Line Knot this once had a
practical application but now can be used as a
decorative formation.

1 Make an overhand loop in the centre of the rope.

2 Form a second overhand loop to the left of the
first loop and then an underhand loop to the right.

3 Move the left loop over the edge of the central
loop to overlap and move the right loop under the
adjacent edge of the centre loop to overlap.

4 Draw these edges of the right and left loop further into the middle of the centre loop so that the
edge of the right loop overlaps the edge of the left,
thereby forming a bight at the very centre.

5 Insert the index and middle fingers of the right hand under and then over the turns on the right hand side and the fingers of the left hand over and then under the turns on the left side to take up the rope at the very centre. Draw these outwards simultaneously to form two loops at the side.

6 Manipulate both of these loops and pull on the loop at the top to ensure that there are three loops of equal size, and tighten the formation.

The Turk's Head

The Turk's Head is a particularly attractive knot that can be tied around cylindrical objects of various sizes. It may take a little practice to be able to estimate the amount of cord end that should be allowed to be able to complete the formation.

1 Leaving a long end turn the cord around the object twice. Ensure that the second turn is below the first and tuck the end underneath the first turn.

2 At the opposite point to this cross the turns and draw the end through the bight which has been formed, over the top turn and below the bottom.

3 Weave the end up through the first turn and down through the first bight (over the top turn and under the bottom). Weave in this way until the knot has been formed.

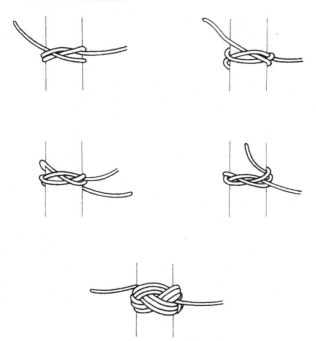

The Monkey's Fist

1 Leave a fairly long end and make three vertical turns with the cord, forming them over the fingers.

2 Hold the vertical turns in place and wind three horizontal turns around them.

3 Draw the end through the space at the bottom and wind the rope in three vertical turns around the horizontal turns, ensuring that the these turns are formed inside the first set of vertical turns.

4 Draw carefully on the standing part to ensure that the knot tightens into a ball shape.

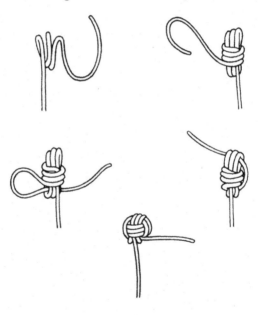

The Figure of Eight Chain

This formation can be used for a decorative cord or strap and can also be used as a fancy shortening.

1 Form a Figure of Eight Knot in the end of the rope but do not draw it completely tight.

2 Follow this with a series of Figure of Eight Knots all formed in the same direction.

3 When a sufficient number of knots have been formed gently draw on the end and the standing part to tighten the knots against one another.

Whipping

Whippings are used to prevent the ends of cut rope from fraying and unravelling. Formed with waxed sailing twine, whipping does not appreciably increase the diameter of the rope, thereby maximizing the rope's utility.

Plain Whipping

Also known as Common Whipping this is a relatively quick, straightforward method for preventing unravelling.

1 Form a bight in the standing part of the twine and hold this firmly against the rope, with the bight facing towards the end.

2 Take up the end of the twine and wind it tightly around the rope and the bight, working against the direction of the lay and towards the end of the rope.

Whipping

3 Once enough turns have been made tuck the end of the twine into the bight and pull on the standing part to tighten the whipping. Trim both ends of the twine to shorten them, but not so short that they will work themselves loose.

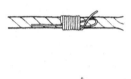

Sailmaker's Whipping

This is a neater form than the Plain Whipping but it needs to be formed with a thick curved sailmaker's needle and some form of thick protective covering for the hands.

1 Make two stitches through the rope with the twine to fix the end.

2 Wind the twine around the rope several times until it is roughly the diameter of the rope itself. Ensure that the stitches are covered by the turns.

3 Draw the end of the twine through the turns and pull it free.

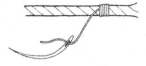

4 Draw the end over the turns and make an angled stitch in the rope.

5 Turn the rope by a third and bring the end over the whipping to make another angled stitch.

6 Repeat this once more so that three stitches are made at roughly a third of the rope circumference away from one another.

7 Repeat the process a second time, on this occasion to double up each of the three stitches.

8 Stitch the twine through twice more and trim the end.

Heat Sealing

This involves the application of extreme heat or a flame to rope composed of a synthetic material. The yarn of the rope will then melt leaving a plug of plastic at the rope end. This is not recommended for working ropes because the plastic can be very rigid and hard and if passed at speed may cause serious injury. Additionally heat sealing may be difficult to learn at first and practice may result in causing damage to the rope.

Seizing

Seizing is the term used to describe a lashing to hold two ropes or two parts of a rope together with thin cord.

Round Seizing

1 Splice an eye in the cord and take the end around both ropes and through the eye.
2 Repeat the turns around both ropes up to ten times, pulling each turn taut. After the final turn has been made draw the end under the turns and pull it free above the bottom turn.

Seizing

3 Make a second series of turns over the first layer but do not pull them quite as taut. Push the end beneath the last two turns on the first layer.

4 Draw the end between the two ropes and make two horizontal 'crossing' turns over the formation to hold it in place.

5 Pull these turns taut and form a Clove Hitch. Turn the end around one of the ropes three or four times and secure it with twine.

Flat Seizing

This is similar to the Round Seizing but without the second layer of 'riding' turns. After the initial layer of turns has been completed the vertical crossing turns are made and the formation finished off by the method described for Round Seizing.

Racking Seizing

This is used when one of the lines is subject to considerable tension.

1 Splice an eye in the cord and pass the end around the ropes and back through the eye.

2 Make up to 15 figure of eight turns around the ropes and use a marline spike to pull them taut.

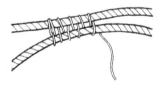

3 Make a second layer of turns to fit in between the first layer and then make vertical cross turns as with the Round Seizing.

4 Finish the formation with the method described for Round Seizing.

Splices

Splicing is a general term given for the method of joining rope or line by unravelling the ends and separating the strands and then tucking these strands into the strands of the rope. Splicing is made with the aid of various instruments, including fids and marline spikes. In addition the ends of the ropes are fixed in two ways by heat sealing whereby the strands of synthetic ropes and lines can be sealed with a match or a red-hot knife, or whipping whereby a twine or a lighter-weight line is turned about the end of a rope several times to prevent further fraying.

Splicing is particularly important in sailing because a knot, particularly if wet, will increase both the diameter and the weight of a rope and will also reduce its breaking strength; a heavy knot is also potentially dangerous. Splices are also formed in wire, particularly on sails where maintaining the rigidity of a line and avoiding slack are of prime importance.

Splicing methods vary according to the construction of the rope. In this section a few of the less complicated splices are described but it is worthwhile examining the types of rope construction that are currently used in sailing.

Splices

Three-strand twisted rope—probably the most economical type of rope which is commonly used for anchoring and mooring. The synthetic fibres are spun into yarns which are then twisted into three strands.

Braided rope with a three-strand core—commonly used for running rigging on yachts, the strength of this rope is sustained in the core. The braided plait cover makes the rope easier to handle and is manufactured in different colours which enables lines to be differentiated easily.

Braided rope with a parallel core—a particularly strong, inelastic rope which is ideal for use as a halyard. The strength of the rope is retained in the core.

Double braid rope—combines a braided sheath cover with a braided hollow core. This necessitates very careful construction of the rope to ensure that the rope strength is sustained equally by the cover and the core. A relatively expensive rope to use, it is vital that care is taken when splicing to ensure that the careful structure of the rope is not disturbed.

Square braid—a rope of eight strands which are plaited into right-laid and left-laid pairs (and usually colour-coded to differentiate). Square braid is commonly used in commercial sailing.

Twelve plait rope—is frequently used for towing and mooring.

The Short Splice (on a three-strand twisted rope)

This is a strong splice but it has the disadvantage of appreciably increasing the diameter of the rope. It cannot, therefore, be used on rope that it is to be passed through a sheave or a block. It is useful for joining two lines together and for mooring.

1 Unlay the strands of the ropes and lay them so that they are equidistant to one another. Tape or heat seal the ends of the strands.

2 Temporarily lash one set of the strands with a thin twine.

Splices

3 Beginning with any of the strands on the other line tuck it over one strand and under one strand of the opposing rope, against the lay of the rope. Then take up the remaining strands and tuck them in the same way.

4 Remove the lashing (known as the 'stop') and then take up one of the strands and tuck into the opposing rope in the manner described above. Repeat this with the remaining two strands.

5 Using a marline spike or a fid to ease open spaces between the strands of the rope, continue to tuck the strands in along the rope.

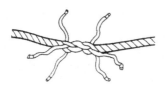

6 When each strand becomes too short to tuck in again trim of the ends, though not too tightly or this may cause them to work themselves free.

The Eye Splice (on a three-strand twisted rope)

This is frequently used for creating a loop in the end of a rope which will be useful in fitting into eyes and grommets since there is no loose end left in the formation.

Splices

1 Unlay the strands of the rope and seal or tape the end of each one. Tape or lash the point at which the unlay ends.
2 Take up the middle strand and tuck this under one strand of the rope above. This should be tucked in against the lay.

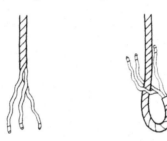

3 Take up the first end and tuck this under the next strand of the rope.

4 Turn the formation over at this point, take up the last end and tuck this under the next strand.

5 Repeat this process twice more before trimming the ends (again do not cut them too closely).
6 The ends of the strands can be heat sealed after they have been trimmed, although care should be taken to ensure that this does not damage the rope in the process.

The Ring Splice (on a three strand twisted rope)

This attaches the working end of a rope to a ring.

1 Unlay the rope 2–3 inches (about 5–7.5 cm) and whip the rope at the base of the unlay. Also whip or seal the ends of each unlayed strand.
2 Pass the strands over the ring and take each strand and pass it back through the ring to lie on the same side as the rope.
3 Take the right-hand strand and turn it around itself once.

4 Remove the whipping at the base of the unlay and take up the middle strand. Tuck this strand under the first strand of the rope, ensuring that it is not part of the right-hand strand which will lie just above.

The Ring Splice (on a three strand twisted rope)

5 Take up the left-hand strand and tuck it under the strand below.

6 Turn the splice over and take up the right-hand strand and tuck it under the next strand down.

7 Continue in this way with each of the strands twice more before trimming the ends.

The Rope to Wire Splice

Used on a braided rope with a three strand core this splice is ideal for attaching ropes to a halyard.

1 Take up the braided fibre rope and form a slip knot about six feet from the end. Push the coat of the rope about four feet up the rope to expose the core of three strands. Cut off a few inches of the core at the end and then whip or tape the end.

2 Tape the core again about 20 inches (approximately 50 cm) from the end.

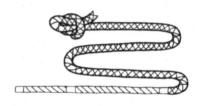

3 Take up the wire rope and begin to taper it by cutting one strand at 6 inches from the end; another strand at 5 inches from the end; a third strand at 4 inches from the end and two strands at 3 inches from the end. Apply tape around the wire at each stage of the tapering.

4 Insert the wire into the core at the end of the fibre

rope at an angle of 45° and continue to work it into the lay of the fibre rope. Tape the wire in position.

5 From the point at which the wire is taped in position (about 6 inches from the end) unlay the strands of the fibre rope.

6 Insert a fid under two of the wire strands against the lay of the wire and pull one of the strands through the groove until it is tight and remove the fid.

7 Repeat this process with the other two strands of fibre rope under a different two strands of the wire rope each time.

8 Repeat the whole process with all three strands up to five times more and then trim the ends very closely.

Splices

9 Gently hold the coat of the braided rope just below the slip knot and section by section work it very gently downwards without actually pulling on the coat.

10 Whip the coat over the point at which the splice ends on the core.

11 Once whipped unravel the coat and divide the yarns equally into three groups. Then splice the yarns into the wire in the direction of the wire lay. Repeat the splicing tucks using one less yarn at each stage until only eight yarns are remaining in each group.

12 Cut the end of the yarns close to the wire to complete the splice.

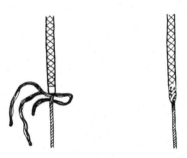

The Eye Splice (on a braided rope with a three-strand core)

1 Form a Slip Knot at about 5 feet (approximately 1.5 metres) from the end; this will prevent the outer braided sheath from unravelling too far upwards.

2 Allow 8–10 inches (approximately 20–25 cm) for the end of the rope and mark this point. Bend the end backwards to form a bight.

3 Measure on another 8–10 inches from the first mark and push apart the threads from the braided coat until the three strand core can be extracted (a fid is ideal for hooking out the strands).

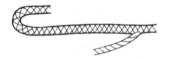

4 Cut of 2–3 inches (approximately 5–7.5 cm) off the end of the core and unlay the three strands.

5 Begin to taper the strands by cutting off one strand and then cutting away at the yarns of

another strand to leave it at half its original thickness. The core should be reduced to a diameter that can be passed through a splicing tool.

6 Take up the splicing tool and insert the eye through the coat at the point at which the core protrudes from the coat. Push it back along towards the end pull it through the coat at the first 8–10 inch marker.

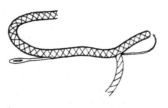

7 Thread the core through the eye of the splicing tool and pull the tool back again so that the core emerges from the original opening.

176

8 Untape the end of the core and unlay the strands before dividing them again into three groups and taping them. Take up the splicing tool and insert the end through the coat about 12 inches (approximately 30 cm) down from the first marker point. Thread one set of strands through the eye and draw on the splicing tool so that the strands emerge at this 12 inch point.

9 Repeat this with the remaining two strands, drawing them through the braid at approximately measured points of 10 and then 8 inches (25 and 20 cm). Untape the strands when this has been completed.

Splices

10 Pull on the strands to ensure that the core and the eye splice are taut.

11 To tidy the ends of the coat, taper the strands and then insert the eye of the of the splicing tool at a point approximately 3 inches (7.5 cm) along from the neck of the bight and extract it at the neck. Insert some of the strands into the eye and pull them through the coat. Find another point on the rope's circumference and repeat the process. Continue in this way until all the cover strands have been pulled through.

12 Carefully trim the remaining core ends and then manipulate the coat so that it runs smoothly over the core from the splice to the Slip Knot.

Glossary

Autobloc: a device that will lock around a rope and prevent slippage when a load is applied in a particular direction.

Bend: a knot which ties the free ends of two ropes together.

Bight: the slack part of the rope between the end and the standing part.

Block: a cased pulley or grooved roller.

Bollard: a short metal mooring post on a pier or on the deck of a ship.

Breaking Strength: the weight (measured in pounds) that is necessary to break a certain rope.

Cross turn: a vertical turn that is taken around the turns or the lashings on a seizing.

End: the working part of the rope.

Fid: a wooden cone-shaped instrument used for splicing.

Halyard: a rope or wire used to hoist a sail.

Hitch: a knot used to tie a line to a hook, a ring, a post or a spar.

Karabiner: a snaplink device used in climbing.

Lanyard: a knot formation tied on a cord attached to smaller items—it is usually decorative.

Glossary

Lashing: any rope or cord used to secure moveable objects.

Lay: the direction in which the strands of a rope are twisted.

Loop: a knot that is made by the end being folded back onto the standing part to form a loop.

Marlinspike: a steel instrument that is used in splicing to separate the strands in a wire rope.

Prusik: a generic term for a group of climbing knots that are designed to grip onto a thick rope when a load is applied.

Riding turns: a second layer of turns in a seizing formation.

Safety back-up: a back-up system to the main system formation in climbing.

Seizing: a method of lashing two ropes or two parts of a rope together.

Sheave: a grooved roller encased in a block.

Sling: a tape or a rope that is put around an object either to act as an anchor or to haul the object. In climbing an extra loop attachment in the climbing rope can be referred to as a sling.

Snaplink: a metal attachment device used on climbing ropes.

Splice: the method of joining two fabric or wire

ropes (or fabric to wire) by the intertwining of the strands and yarns.

Standing Part: the main part of a line which is not being worked as part of a knot formation.

Strand: the set of twisted yarns.

Twine: a resilient but lightweight line that is used in the formation of seizings, whippings and splices.

Unlay: To untwist the lay of a three strand rope and separate the individual strands.

Whipping: the method of binding the end of rope with twine to prevent it from unravelling.

Index

Index

Index

Index